MOSQUITO

i

by Jerry Scutts

Color by Don Greer
Illustrated by Tom Tullis

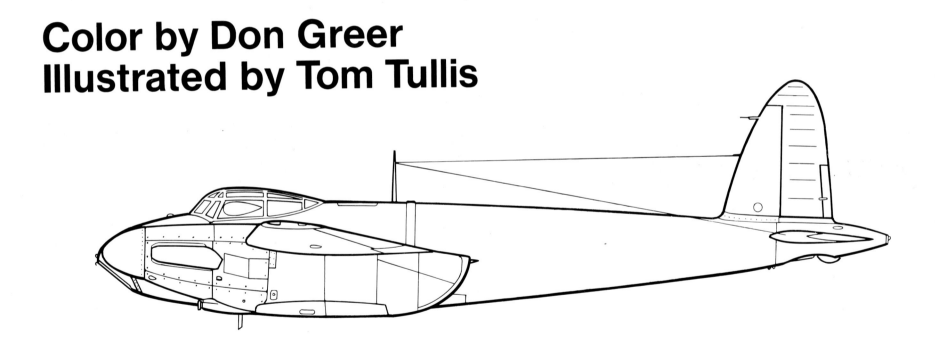

Aircraft Number 127
squadron/signal publications

A Mosquito B Mk IV of No 139 Squadron flies low over the English Channel enroute to targets along the French coast. No 139 Squadron was based at Horsham Saint Faith and was the second RAF unit to receive the Mosquito B IV.

ISBN 0-89747-283-7

If you have any photographs of the aircraft, armor, soldiers or ships of any nation, particularly wartime snapshots, why not share them with us and help make Squadron/Signal's books all the more interesting and complete in the future. Any photograph sent to us will be copied and the original returned. The donor will be fully credited for any photos used. Please send them to:

Squadron/Signal Publications, Inc.
1115 Crowley Drive.
Carrollton, TX 75011-5010.

Photo Credits

Bruce Robertson	Philip Jarrett
RAF Museum	Robert F. Dorr
Imperial War Museum	Frank Marshall
Harry Holmes	Aeroplane Monthly
W. Gill	J. Stewart
Owen Thetford	Dave Howley
Weeks Air Museum	Larry Davis
Air Force Museum	Nicholas J. Waters III

Note: This volume covers the bomber, photo reconnaissance and special use variants of the Mosquito. Part II will cover the fighter, fighter-bomber and trainer variants.

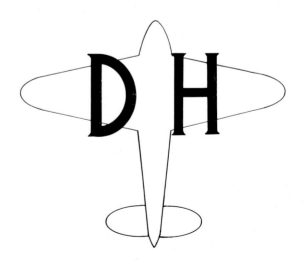

A pair of No 105 Squadron Mosquito B IV bombers fly in formation over a solid undercast shortly after the unit re-equipped with the de Havilland bomber during November of 1941. (RAF Museum)

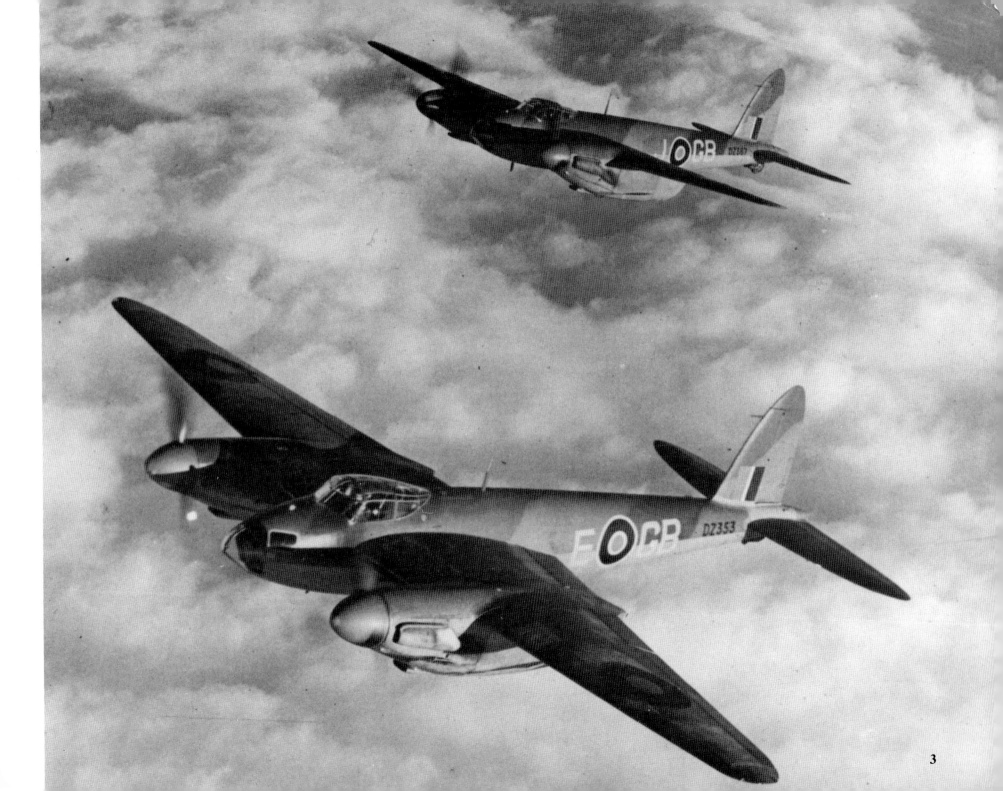

3

Introduction

Nearly fifty years after the end of the most destructive war in history, veterans of WW II still recall the finer points of the aircraft they flew. The passage of time probably makes them remember the aircraft's good qualities far more then the bad points and that is quite understandable. A lot would also depend on the aircraft being recalled. If it was the de Havilland Mosquito, there weren't many bad qualities to begin with! The "Mossie" is still held in high esteem by the British, Dominion and American aircrews who were fortunate enough to fly this superlative warplane.

Stories told of the Mosquito are legion, but some are particularly appropriate. There was the time when a B-26 Marauder crew met a Mosquito over England. The "word" had gotten around that de Havilland had developed a bomber that was faster than most fighters, let alone bombers. The B-26 crew was not convinced and a race of sorts resulted. They knew that their ship had a high top speed and the anonymous RAF crew were not at all bashful about accepting the challenge. The Marauder crew soon wished they hadn't been so bold. The B-26 was pounding along, throttles through the firewall, when the Mossie hammered past, inverted and flying on one engine.

A fair number of books have already been written of the exploits of Mosquito crews, who became a thorn in the side of the Germans and Japanese alike. The Mosquito was built in a variety of variants including fighter, bomber, reconnaissance, transport, trainer, target tug and test bed. Not only did the Mosquito contribute significantly to the Allied victory but it also gave the RAF an aircraft that linked the pre-war designed four-engined heavy bombers with the light, fast tactical bombers that became the primary strike aircraft of the jet age. So versatile was the Mosquito that the main criticism from all commands was that there were never enough to go around.

The origins of the Mosquito can be traced back to 1935, when initial studies were undertaken by the Royal Aircraft Establishment to produce a modern twin-engined bomber with fighter performance. Among the ideas studied was an aircraft powered by two Rolls Royce engines with turret guns for defense. An alternative variant of this design was completely unarmed and was estimated to be fast enough to evade enemy fighters by speed alone.

The Mosquito mock-up under construction at Salisbury Hall, Hertfordshire, England during June of 1940. The design team had to work in the cramped single bay hangar because space at the de Havilland main plant could not be spared from priority wartime production programs. (Bruce Robertson)

On 24 August 1936, Air Ministry Specification P.13/36 was issued to the British aviation industry. Optimistic and rather too general in its requirements, it called for a twin-engined medium bomber capable of carrying a 1,000 pound bomb load for at least 1,000 miles at 15,000 feet. Catapult takeoff (which seemed to offer some advantages in getting heavy aircraft airborne from short, grass runways) was to be allowed for and this was estimated to boost the bomb load to 4,000 pounds and the range to 3,000 miles.

It was the specified cruising speed of 275 mph which proved to be the major stumbling block and, in the event, none of the proposed designs was able to meet this requirement. Despite the fact that de Havilland's submission was based on the use of two Rolls Royce Merlin liquid cooled inline engines, it had an estimated top speed of only 260 mph with a 4,000 pound projected bomb load and a 1,500 mile range. To meet the speed requirement, more power was needed.

To keep the company viable through the lean inter-war years, de Havilland had designed and built a series of civil aircraft for both the sport market and the airlines. Air racing had given the company useful experience in building streamlined airframes and the DH Albatross airliner was one of the most aerodynamically clean four-engined aircraft to enter service.

The idea of a new combat aircraft was shelved, but not forgotten, and in 1938 a twin Merlin powered design, based on the Albatross, was submitted. This too proved unsatisfactory in performance, as did a derivative of the Flamingo airliner. It was felt that all the previous design studies used too large an airframe and that a smaller aircraft powered by two Merlins, would offer the performance that de Havilland and the Air Ministry sought.

Achieving high speed meant keeping airframe weight to a minimum and, with war with Germany looming, de Havilland again opted to construct the new airframe largely of wood. Wood had been used successfully on both the Albatross airliner and DH 88 Comet racer and would have significant advantages if the impending war meant shortages, particularly in aircraft grade aluminum and other strategic materials needed for conventional aircraft. Also, a sizeable industry then engaged on furniture manufacture could, it was believed, be converted to build airframes to the high tolerances needed.

It was the intended lack of armament that probably caused the most doubts about de Havilland's ideas in official circles. Fighter speeds were advancing all the time and it was feared, with some justification, that the high speed bomber would soon be overtaken by advances in fighter design. Not to be swayed, de Havilland submitted two final design studies in September of 1939, both based on the twin Merlin layout and both having an estimated top speed nearly 400 mph. Backed by Air Marshal Sir Wilfred Freeman, Air Member for Research, the project was kept alive throughout the early weeks of the Second World War and on 12 December 1939, a prototype was ordered by the Air Ministry.

With the speed, bomb load and range figures finally acceptable to the Air Ministry, DH project No 98 formed the basis of Specification B.1/40. This specification, written around the de Havilland proposal, called for a reconnaissance/bomber aircraft weighing less than 20,000 pounds in both configurations with a maximum speed of 397 mph and a service ceiling of 32,100 feet.

On 5 October 1940, the design team moved five miles from the DH plant at Hatfield to the relative safety of Salisbury Hall, a stately home with grounds large enough to accommodate the workshops necessary to build the prototype. Ronald E. Bishop was the chief designer, assisted by W. A. Tamblin, senior designer and Richard M. Clarkson, head of aerodynamics.

Before the prototype DH 98 was completed, the Air Ministry placed an initial production order, on 1 March 1940, for fifty bomber/reconnaissance aircraft. This heartening news was offset by the imminent fear of invasion and an official ban on any aviation project that interrupted the manufacture of first line fighters, bombers and trainers. DH became involved in such desperate measures as the production of bomb racks for Tiger Moth biplane trainers and, Lord Beaverbrook, newly-appointed head of the Ministry of Aircraft Production, forbade resources being diverted into any work not geared at keeping the Germans from crossing the Channel. On three separate occasions, the Mosquito was faced with cancellation.

The Hatfield factory was fully occupied with war work, not the least of which was the conversion of DH propellers from fixed to constant pitch and Merlin engine repair. But with the Battle of Britain won and the immediate threat of a German invasion postponed, the Fall of 1940 saw the Mosquito prototype roll out at Salisbury Hall. Having convinced Beaverbrook that work on the prototype did not interrupt Hatfield's output, construction work had gone ahead steadily and in November, the prototype (W4050) was moved by road to the DH plant for final assembly.

Taxi trials were carried out on 24 November and on the following day, the overall Yellow prototype, with the manufacturer's Class B registration E0234, took off on its maiden flight. Chief Test Pilot Geoffrey de Havilland, Jr. was at the controls, while John Walker, in charge of engine installation, occupied the right seat. For thirty minutes the aircraft was put through its paces and when it landed, there was little doubt that the superbly streamlined prototype had unsurpassed potential as a combat aircraft.

The DH 98 was built around a fifty-two foot six inch, one piece, two spar wing which kept weight to a minimum. The box spars were made of spruce, with plywood webs and plywood skinning. The center section of the wing carried the engine mounts, which were of welded steel tubing, and the radiators, which protruded forward of the wing leading edge by twenty-two inches. This feature freed the short nacelles from any drag-inducing radiator fairing. Wood was also used for the flaps, although the ailerons were of light alloy.

Built in two halves, the wooden fuselage was joined along the centerline once all the control runs were in place. The large cutout for the wing was sealed with an underside fuselage section once the wing was attached (via four heavy-duty pick-up points). The wood tail unit had an aluminum, fabric covered rudder and elevators. Both landing gear legs were interchangeable, precious metal being saved by the use of compressed rubber blocks rather than oleo-pneumatic shock absorbers. The tailwheel was retractable but not enclosed by doors.

That de Havilland had produced an exceptional aircraft became increasingly apparent as the prototype was put thorough a series of test flights in advance of the official RAF acceptance. The prototype even weathered a damaging crash at Boscombe Down. The crash had a hidden bonus, for de Havilland company engineers were able to repair the broken fuselage in the field, demonstrating the ease with which a damaged Mosquito could be put back into service.

The only adverse characteristic that came to light during pre-service testing was some tail buffeting, caused by disturbed airflow aft of the engine nacelles. This trouble was cured on later production aircraft by lengthening the nacelle so that it projected beyond the wing trailing edge.

The Mosquito prototype was painted overall Yellow as a safety measure to ensure local anti-aircraft gunners would not fire on the aircraft during its test flights. The Class B registration E0234 denoted that the aircraft was a private venture, not a government-funded prototype. (Robertson)

Development

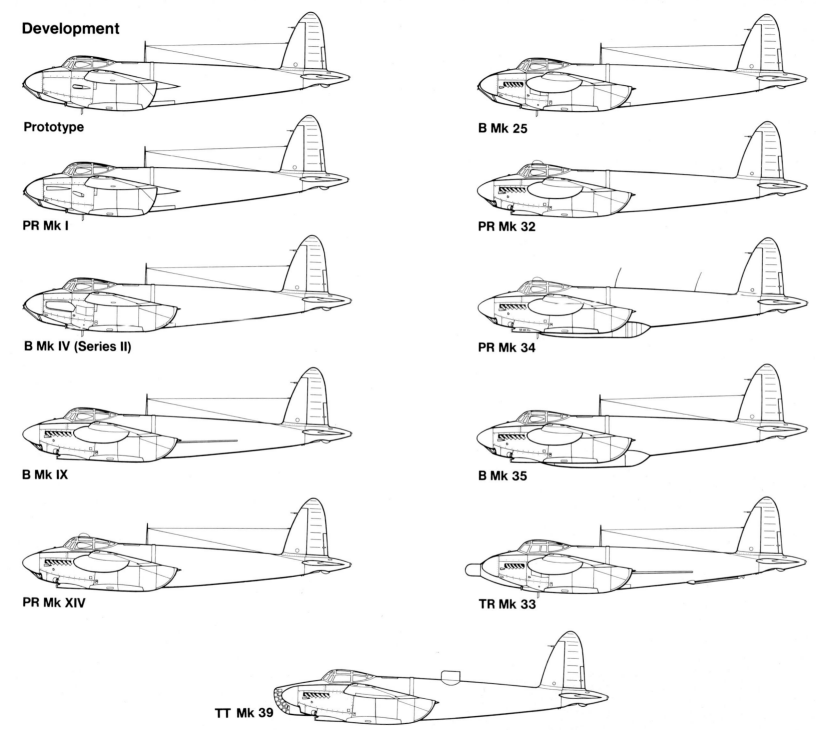

Prototype

PR Mk I

B Mk IV (Series II)

B Mk IX

PR Mk XIV

B Mk 25

PR Mk 32

PR Mk 34

B Mk 35

TR Mk 33

TT Mk 39

Mosquito PR Mk I

On 30 December 1940, the Air Ministry ordered a further 150 Mosquitoes and de Havilland set about establishing a network of sub-contractors to meet the orders that they had on hand (which now totaled some 200 aircraft). In the meantime, the prototype began testing new engines and systems that would be incorporated into future production Mosquitoes.

A fighter version had been ordered in July of 1940 (Mosquito F Mk II) and among the armament options investigated was a four gun turret behind the cockpit. Luckily, this arrangement was dropped in favor of a combined machine gun/cannon installation in the forward fuselage.

The prototype reconnaissance Mosquito PR Mk I (W4051) flew for the first time on 10 June 1941. It differed from the Mosquito prototype in having twenty inch longer wings (fifty-four feet two inch wing span) and in the camera installation, which normally consisted of three vertical cameras (F24, F52, or K17) and one oblique (F24) camera mounted in the lower fuselage. The camera arrangement varied depending on the mission. One of the most common was a single K17 6 inch focal length camera forward and a split vertical F52 20 or 36 inch installation behind the wing and an F24 14 inch oblique mounted camera firing to port. This was sometimes changed to a split vertical F52 20 or 36 inch camera installation forward, two standard vertical F52 cameras and one oblique F24 camera behind the wing. The F24 camera could use either a 5 inch, 8 inch, 14 inch (most widely used) or 24 inch lens depending on the scale of photography desired and area to be covered. The split vertical camera installation was basically two cameras (F24s or F52s) mounted at slightly differing angles to double the field of view, yet retaining the sixty percent overlap needed for steroscopic coverage of the target area. The split vertical F52 36 inch camera installation gave the Mosquito PR Mk I lateral coverage of some three miles from 35,000 feet and 255 mph. From 24,000 feet, the cameras produced such high quality photographs that interpreters were able to distinguish the markings on the float aircraft carried aboard the German cruiser PRINZ EUGEN.

The Mosquito PR Mk I prototype (W4051) saw operational service with the pioneer Photographic Development Unit, later redesignated as No 1 Photographic Reconnaissance Unit, at Benson. The aircraft carried the identification code LY-U. (Philip Jarrett)

At first the camera mounts were made of steel, but these were later changed to wooden mounts since these helped reduce camera vibration and improve image quality. The PR Mk I retained the short engine nacelles and tailplane of the original prototype. The PR Mk I prototype was delivered to No 1 Photographic Reconnaissance Unit at Benson on 13 July and by mid-September it had been joined by four production Mosquito PR Mk Is. Over the course of their operations, two of the unit's PR Mk Is were modified with increased fuel tankage for long range operations.

Camera Installations

Mosquito PR Mk I

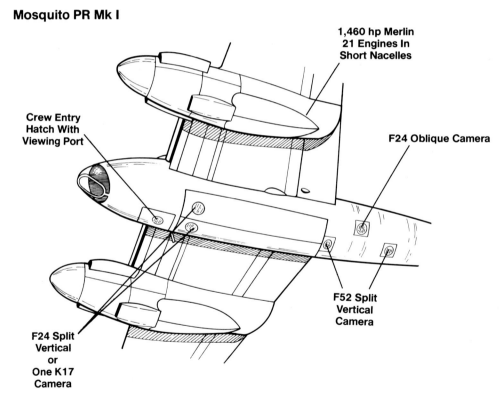

1,460 hp Merlin 21 Engines In Short Nacelles

Crew Entry Hatch With Viewing Port

F24 Oblique Camera

F52 Split Vertical Camera

F24 Split Vertical or One K17 Camera

From the beginning, the Mosquito PR Mk I carried a unique color scheme, overall PRU Blue. This Blue-Gray camouflage had been arrived at after extensive experimentation (mostly with PR Spitfires) and was felt to be ideal for the high flying reconnaissance aircraft.

The initial order for fifty aircraft was changed before production was fully started to nineteen PR Mk I aircraft (plus the prototype PR Mk I) and twenty-eight F Mk II fighters, along with a fighter prototype. This changing of the variants on order, while a tribute to the Mosquito's versatility, did have some detrimental effects on production schedules and led to a delay in the aircraft's entry to service.

A further delay was caused by the time it took to establish a reliable network of sub-contractors who could work to the standards required for airframe manufacture. This was far from easy but it had to be done as Hatfield was occupied during 1941 with the completion of no less than 800 Oxford trainers. In the long term, it was felt that alternative manufacturers for future trainer orders was the best solution so that de Havilland could concentrate on Mosquito production.

Eventually, some 400 firms would contribute to the Mosquito program, but some idea of the difficulty faced by de Havilland in finding the right sub-contractors was shown by the fact that some 10,000 drawings and schedules were needed for the DH 89, while only 1,400 were needed for a Tiger Moth trainer. A further modification of the early production orders (on 17 July 1941) had brought a bomber variant into the picture, with nine of the twenty PR Mk Is on order now being completed as bombers.

The first combat mission by a Mosquito was carried out by a PR Mk I on 17 September 1941 when Squadron Leader R. Clerke flying W4055 made the first photo run over enemy territory, successfully photographing Brest and the Franco-German frontier. During the mission, he successfully evaded three Bf 109s which tried to intercept him. In a short time, much of Western Europe came under the scrutiny of the high flying Benson based Mosquitoes, with sorties to East Prussia and Augsburg in Bavaria being among the longest of the war to date.

Powered by two 1,460 hp Merlin 21 engines, the PR Mk I could fly further (2,180 miles), faster (382 mph) and higher (35,000 feet) than anything else then available. As a result, the Mosquito was naturally in great demand by No 1 PRU. The low production run of only ten PR Mk Is led Benson to "scrounge" another two aircraft (originally earmarked as fighters) to be followed by two more similar machines.

The Mosquito PR Mk I prototype (W4051) was delivered on 13 July 1941. At the time few people realized the importance of the event to the RAF's future conduct of the war. PR Mosquitoes had the speed and range to allow the RAF to build the pre and post strike target intelligence files needed for offensive operations.

Mosquito B Mk IV

The nine early production bomber variants diverted from the first order for PR Mk I aircraft (W4064 to W4072) were known as Mosquito B Mk IV Series Is, both to distinguish them from later production bombers ordered and built as bombers (Series II aircraft) and to denote the fact that they had the same short engine nacelles as used on the prototype and PR Mk I.

The bomb load of the Mosquito B Mk IV Series I had been established at a modest 1,000 pounds, a figure arrived at by using standard production British bombs. Production Mosquito bombers were to have been designated as Mk Vs, but only one example, W4057, was built. Tests with this aircraft revealed that it was possible to double the bomb load. Boscombe Down's technicians found that if the fins of the standard 500 pound bomb could be shortened, the Mosquito bomb bay could take four of them. Telescopic fins, which extended once the bomb was clear of the aircraft, were successfully tested but drop tests proved that a shortened bomb fin had no detrimental effect on the standard bomb and this was far simpler solution.

The Series II aircraft differed from the earlier Series I aircraft mainly in the engine nacelles. To cure the airflow problems around the nacelle it was extended beyond the wing trailing edge. Additionally, the wheel well doors were enlarged and the exhaust system was changed to individual exhaust stacks which were covered by a shroud to hide the exhaust flame for night operations.

The wing was modified to accept underwing 50 gallon slipper type drop tanks outboard of the engine nacelle which became a standard fitting. With production of the B Mk IV (Series II) underway, service entry took place as soon as adequate stocks of short-finned 500 pound bombs had been built up. On 15 November 1941, Geoffrey de Havilland delivered W4064 to No 105 Squadron at Swanton Morley — the kind of personal service that other manufacturers had not provided!

Later, further tests into bomb carrying capability were flown by a Mk IV (DK290/G) which served as a bomber development aircraft. Among the tests was one aimed at improving performance by fitting wing root fillets and giving the airframe a high polish; another test involved the Highball anti-ship bomb and still others were flown to confirm the Mosquito's suitability as a mine-laying aircraft.

The Mosquito was to be used in a variety of combat roles. The Mk IV bomber prototype (W4057, later the Mk V prototype) is overflown by the overall Black F Mk II fighter prototype (W4052). The Yellow P marking on the fuselage identified the aircraft as a prototype.

Mosquitoes found an almost unique role in Bomber Command, even before the days of the Path Finder Force (PFF). It was thought that if the new de Havilland twin was sent over major enemy targets in small numbers, it would wear down morale by keeping the defenses alerted around the clock. On 1 June 1942, the unfortunate citizens of Cologne heard the wail of air raid sirens less than twenty-four hours after the RAF had raided the city with more than 1,000 heavy bombers. Screaming over Cologne at low level, a quartet of No 105 Squadron Mosquitoes dropped their loads and departed as quickly as they had come. For the Germans, it was a taste of things to come.

An even more significant raid took place on 26 September when No 105 Squadron was tasked to destroy a single building in Oslo, Norway. This began what amounted to almost a private war against the Gestapo by Mosquito crews. Using four aircraft, the squadron went in at low level and put bombs through the roof of the Gestapo Headquarters building to destroy vital dossiers on Norwegian resistance personnel. The raid cost the squadron one Mosquito which was shot down by intercepting Fw 190s. Raids like this made the Mossie synonymous with pin-point attacks on tiny targets, often from very low level.

No 139 Squadron became the second Mosquito bomber unit on 8 June 1942, the unit initially using No 105 Squadron's aircraft and personnel resources. These two units honed the Mosquito bomber and developed tactics for its use. It was found that while the de Havilland bomber could show even the Fw 190 a clean pair of heels, the speed margin it enjoyed was small. More tests were conducted to try to get the last ounce of speed out of the airframe. Although airframe polishing and the deletion of anything that would interrupt the airflow gained a few miles per hour, it was found that an improved exhaust system was needed to give the Mosquitoes a worthwhile ten to twelve mph more speed.

Engine Nacelles

B Mk IV Series I

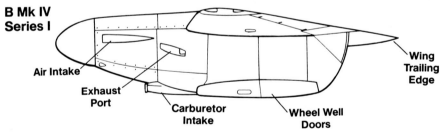

Air Intake
Exhaust Port
Carburetor Intake
Wheel Well Doors
Wing Trailing Edge

B Mk IV Series II

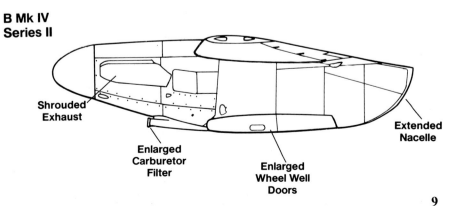

Shrouded Exhaust
Enlarged Carburetor Filter
Enlarged Wheel Well Doors
Extended Nacelle

Ejector exhaust stacks with oval section ends gave an improved "jet" effect when compared with the standard "saxophone" stacks with the flame damping exhaust shroud. As a result, some bombers had these stacks fitted and the shrouds deleted. It was thought to be unwise, however, to advertise the Mosquito's presence by removing the flame dampers and, for dawn and dusk attacks, most B IVs retained the shrouds.

Disrupting enemy war potential was of paramount importance, but hurting Nazi prestige in the eyes of the faithful was also an attractive prospect for the RAF. On 30 January 1943, a mission was planned where Mosquito crews would be unwelcomed guests at a Nazi party rally in Berlin. At 1100, right on schedule, three Mosquito B IVs of No 105 Squadron forced Reichmarschall Goring to postpone his speech. Just before 1600 that afternoon, No 139 Squadron raided the city, abruptly cutting off an address by Dr. Goebbels. It was the first successful attack on Berlin by Mosquitoes and flight times, enemy defenses and other information was carefully noted for future reference.

In May of 1943, Nos 105 and 139 Squadrons were posted from No 2 Group to No 8 Path Finder Force (PFF) Group to develop new tactics for the night bomber offensive against Germany. On 26 June, Mosquitoes made their operational debut with the navigational aid Gee and that November, Mosquitoes began dropping Window on "Spoof" raids, which became an integral part of future operations.

By early 1944, Nos 627 and 692 Squadrons had joined 8 Group, following trials with the radar aid, Oboe by No 109 Squadron. Using a B Mk IV (DK300) for the initial installation (on 21 July 1942), the squadron used the new devices for the first time on 20 December for a raid on a Dutch power station.

An important boost to the Mosquito's offensive capability was made in April of 1943 when work began on modifications to the B Mk IV to enable it to carry a 4,000 pound bomb. Using DZ594/G, the manufacturers were pleased, and perhaps a little surprised, that the big bomb pushed the Mosquito's all-up weight to 21,500 pounds, about four times the payload that had originally been thought possible.

Although the Mosquito could easily lift a "Cookie," it was notably unstable, and flying on one engine with the bomb was not recommended. To carry the bomb it was necessary to bulge the bomb bay doors and to add some sixty pounds of ballast to the nose to improve the aircraft's stability. Additionally, the elevators were modified with horn balances. The main fuel tankage was reduced and the twenty-three B IVs modified to carry the 4,000 pound bomb normally flew with two 50 gallon underwing slipper type drop tanks. The first operational use of Mosquitoes using 4,000 pound "Cookies" took place on 23 February 1944 when three No 692 Squadron B IVs attacked Dusseldorf.

Another modified Mosquito Mk IV was used by No 618 Squadron. Formed originally to carry two of Barnes Wallis's "Bouncing" bombs, similar to the "Upkeep" weapons used by No 617 Squadron's Lancasters for the May 1943 Ruhr dams raid. The smaller Highball was designed for Mosquito use and it was planned that No 618 would attack the battleship TIRPITZ using these weapons. Delays in the production of the special bombs, code named Highball, and official fears that greater use of such revolutionary munitions would lead to them being copied by the enemy, served to keep the mission on ice.

A Mosquito B Mk IV Series II (in the foreground) shares the ramp with an FB Mk IV, two other B Mk IVs and an NF Mk II. All these aircraft have one thing in common: serials in the DZ range. A total of 300 B IV Series IIs were completed.

Exhaust System
(Shroud Removed)

B Mk IV Series II (Early)

B Mk IV Series II (Late)

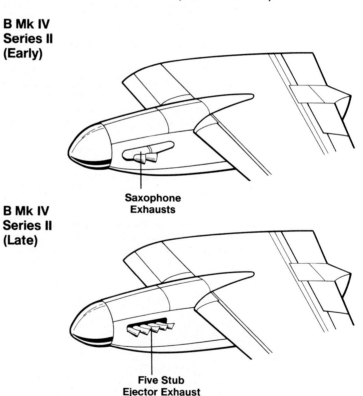

Saxophone Exhausts

Five Stub Ejector Exhaust

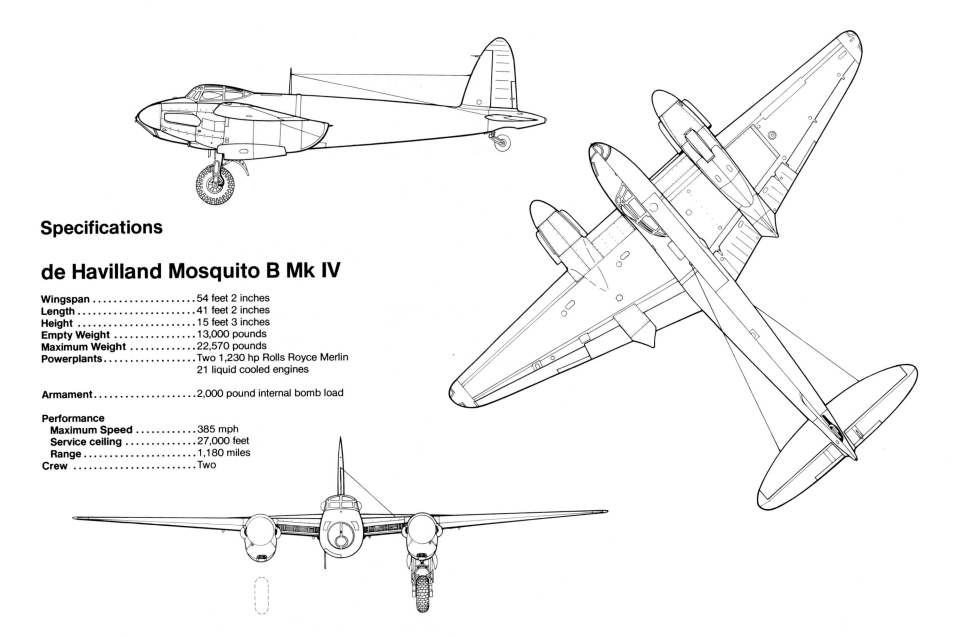

Specifications

de Havilland Mosquito B Mk IV

Wingspan .54 feet 2 inches
Length . . . . .41 feet 2 inches
Height . . . . .15 feet 3 inches
Empty Weight . . . . .13,000 pounds
Maximum Weight . . . . .22,570 pounds
Powerplants . . . . .Two 1,230 hp Rolls Royce Merlin
21 liquid cooled engines

Armament .2,000 pound internal bomb load

Performance
  Maximum Speed . . . . .385 mph
  Service ceiling . . . . .27,000 feet
  Range . . . . .1,180 miles
Crew . . . . .Two

Nevertheless, No 618 Squadron, formed on 1 April 1943 with Mosquito B Mk IVs, trained hard. In July of 1944 unit personnel were told that they would be sent to the Pacific for anti-shipping work, their aircraft being launched from carriers.

Twenty-nine B Mk IVs were delivered by late September, these machines having been modified with arrestor hooks, armored windscreens, Merlin 25 engines driving four blade propellers, a deeper and wider bomb bay to carry the special bombs, a small turbine to spin them before release and the bomb suspension gear. Deployed to Australia on 28 October to prepare for operations against the Japanese, No 618's crews had perfected the technique of hitting ships with their unusual bombs during numerous practice missions. Fully up to strength with twenty-seven B Mk IVs and three PR XVIs, No 618 was destined never to see action and before the end of the war the squadron was disbanded. The special weapons were blown up and the aircraft, apart from two PR XVIs which were transferred to the RAAF, were sold.

The British Overseas Airways Corporation (BOAC) also operated a number of Mosquito B Mk IVs as high speed mail/passenger aircraft for operations between England and Sweden. The aircraft were modified with extra fuel tanks, deicing equipment and additional radio and navigational aids. The aircraft retained their RAF camouflage but carried large civil registration codes on the wings and fuselage, with the fuselage codes underlined with Red/White/Blue stripes.

A total of 300 B Mk IV Series IIs were built.

Mosquito B Mk V

As related earlier, only one Mk V (W4057) was built and this mark number was not taken up for production Mosquitoes.

Mosquito PR Mk IV

Continuing to pioneer the increasingly vital need for reliable photographic coverage of Europe, No 1 PRU at Benson had converted two Mosquito B IVs (DZ411 and DZ419) to the PR Mk IV standard by adding a camera installation similar to that of the PR Mk I in the bomb bay area. A further twenty-seven B Mk IVs were converted for PR work, with additional fuel tanks occupying a part of the bomb bay. These aircraft, along with two other bomber conversions (DK284 and W4066), enabled No 1 PRU to extend its reach into Russia. On 8 July 1942 the unit went out in search of the battleship TIRPITZ, found her and made a refueling stop at Murmansk before flying back to Leuchars.

Greater altitude capability was needed and after the PR Mk IV had discovered evidence of V-2 activity at Peenamunde during mid 1943, the variant was phased out in favor of a new Mosquito variant specially developed for high altitude work. The last PR Mk IV sortie was made on 10 September 1943.

Mosquito PR Mk VIII

To widen the Mosquito's photographic role, a number of interim photo variants were built in small numbers, among them the PR Mk VIII. This mark number covered only five airframes: DK324, DZ342, DZ364, DZ404 and DZ424 (all of which were modified B Mk IVs).

This B Mk IV Series II was named *THE JOKER* and was assigned No 105 Squadron based at Marham, Norfolk and was the first to fly Oboe-equipped Mossies. Most Mosquitoes in the squadron had the four playing card suit insignia painted on the nose and many had individual names.

Without the weight of guns and ammunition, a well maintained Mosquito B Mk IV could outrun enemy fighters. This advantage was put to good use by British Overseas Airways Corporation to maintain a limited fast courier service to Sweden. BOAC operated a total of ten Mosquitoes (seven originally ordered plus three replacement). This Bk Mk IV, G-AGFV, was the first Mossie delivered to BOAC.

Mosquito B Mk VII

The Mosquito B Mk VII was basically a Mosquito B Mk IV that was built in Canada. The first batch of Canadian-built Mosquitoes, production of which was initiated on 7 July 1941, were built at the de Havilland of Canada Limited (DHC) Downsview plant just outside Toronto. One difference between British and Canadian built Mosquitoes was the power plant. Canadian Mosquitoes used American-built Merlin engines supplied by the Packard Car Company of Detroit, Michigan under an agreement made in September of 1940 between Packard and Rolls Royce.

Production drawings were shipped to DHC following a visit to Downsview by two Hatfield engineers and the necessary tools and jigs were dispatched from Britain by sea. Some of these were lost in transit with the result that DHC made a number of its own manufacturing jigs to get production underway using sub-contractors both in Canada and in the U.S.

The first twenty-five Canadian-built airframes, based on the Mosquito B Mk IV, were designated as B Mk VIIs and allocated the serials KB300-KB324. Powered by two 1,390 hp Packard Merlin 31s, the first B VII made its maiden flight on 24 September 1942. When this order was completed, Canadian production switched to variants with mark numbers in the 20 thru 29 range. Six of the B VIIs were later converted to F-8-DH photo reconnaissance aircraft for the USAAF.

A Mosquito B Mk VII (KB300) on a test flight over Canada. Canadian built Mosquitoes were powered by Packard-built Merlin engines, produced in Detroit, Michigan under an agreement between Packard and Rolls Royce. (RCAF via R.F. Dorr)

KB300 was the first Mosquito B MK IV built in Canada by de Havilland of Canada (DHC). A production batch of twenty-four B Mk VIIs (basically a B Mk IV with American built engines) followed, six of which were delivered to the USAAF. (RCAF via R. F. Dorr)

Mosquito B Mk IX

Development of the Mosquito B IX began during 1942 when de Havilland fitted the Mosquito prototype with a pair of 1,680 hp Merlin 61 engines equipped with two-stage superchargers and four blade propellers. On its second test flight, during June of 1942, the aircraft reached an altitude of 40,000 feet, the highest ever reached by a Mosquito.

After its initial testing the prototype was modified, with three blade propellers replacing the four blade propellers which had been found to cause engine surging. The additional power of the Merlin 61 gave the prototype an increased top speed of 432 mph, some 52 mph faster than the B Mk IV. Later the prototype was retrofitted with 1,710 hp Merlin 77 engines, and with these engines W4050 reached 437 mph at 29,000 feet, the highest speed ever achieved by a Mosquito in level flight.

Two-stage Merlin 61 engines became available for installation in production Mosquitoes at the end of 1942 and a production Mosquito was converted to serve as the prototype for the B Mk IX series. It emerged as the first of the high altitude Mosquitoes, although it did not have a pressurized cabin. The first production example (LR495) made its maiden flight on 24 March 1943 and a total of fifty-four B IXs were built, most of which were delivered to Bomber Command squadrons, although a small number were used for the weather reconnaissance role.

The production B IX differed from the earlier B Mk IV in that it was powered by the 1,680 hp Merlin 72 engine (1,505 bhp at 21,000 feet). The use of these supercharged engines made it necessary to modify the engine nacelles. A chin type air intake was added to the front of the nacelle for the supercharger intercooler and the carburetor air intake was deepened. Normally no exhaust shrouds were fitted and these engines had six exhaust stacks instead of the five stacks found on most B Mk IVs.

The Mosquito B Mk IX was powered by 1,680 hp, two-stage, supercharged Merlin 72 engines. Early production B Mk IXs did not feature the bulged bomb bay doors that enabled Mosquitoes to carry the massive 4,000 pound "Cookie" bomb, although a number of aircraft had these door retrofitted. (RAF Museum)

Work had been done aimed at designing a "universal" wing for the Mosquito that would allow the carriage of bombs as well as underwing fuel tanks and the B Mk IX was the first Mosquito bomber to use this wing. The B Mk IX could carry two 500 pound bombs mounted on universal bomb carriers in place of the underwing 50 or 100 gallon fuel tanks. Internally, the B Mk IX could carry another four 500 pound bombs, giving the aircraft a useful load of some 3,000 pounds.

B Mk IXs were also fitted with various electronic bombing aids such as Oboe, Gee-H, and H2S radar. With these aids, the B IXs usually attacked from 30,000 feet, maintaining a speed of 320 mph. No 109 Squadron was the first unit to receive the type, accepting their first aircraft on 21 April 1943.

The original Mosquito prototype (W4050) was later fitted with two-stage supercharged Merlin 61 engines for a series of comparison tests against the Lockheed F-5 Lightning and the Westland Whirlwind fighter-bomber. The tests revealed that the Mosquito was clearly superior to both the F-5 and Whirlwind.

The 1,682 hp Rolls Royce Merlin 72 engines fitted to the B Mk IX had six exhaust stacks instead of the five found on the late B MK IV. The nacelles were also modified with much larger air intakes for the carburetor and supercharger intercooler.

Mosquito PR Mk IX

It was logical that the improved performance of the B Mk IX would be adapted for PR work and, in fact, more PR variants of these were built than bombers — a total of ninety aircraft (against only fifty-four bombers). The first two production aircraft (LR405 and LR406) were delivered to No 540 Squadron in April of 1943. With a warload, the B Mk IX had an internal fuel load of 497 gallons along with two 100 gallon wing tanks, for a total of 697 gallons. But without the need to carry bombs, the PR Mk IX had the useful capacity of 860 gallons, including two fifty gallon drop tanks. Alternatively, two 100 gallon underwing tanks could be fitted, giving the PR Mk IX a total fuel load of over 1,000 gallons.

With such a fuel load, the PR IX was heavy with an absolute maximum (with 100 gallon wing tanks) of 25,160 pounds. Range with underwing tanks was some 2,450 miles at a cruising speed of 250 mph.

As the PR IX became available in useful numbers it was used extensively to cover the German rocket research program, photographing research centers and test sites. During 1943 two Mosquito PR Mk 1Xs were used to test the use of American made M46 photo flash bombs. These were used to illuminate a target for night photography. The M46 was some three times brighter than existing British photo flash bombs and could be carried internally by the Mosquito. Initially there were some problems with the coordinating the cameras and flash bombs but these were solved and, by the Spring of 1943, the system was producing good quality night photographs.

Engine Nacelle

B Mk IV

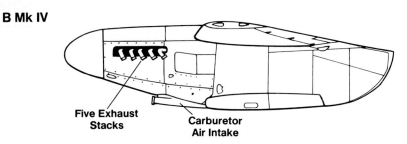

Five Exhaust Stacks

Carburetor Air Intake

B Mk IX/PR Mk IX

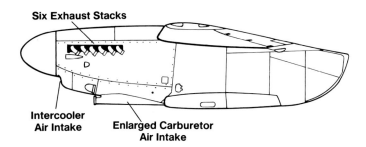

Six Exhaust Stacks

Intercooler Air Intake

Enlarged Carburetor Air Intake

15

Wing Stores

B Mk IV

50 Gallon
Fuel Tank

B Mk IX
PR Mk IX

50/100 Gallon
Fuel Tank or
Universal Carrier

500 Pound Bomb

This Mosquito B Mk IX was named the *The Waltzing Mosquito* and carried the name on the nose in White. This aircraft is also fitted with cockpit side window blisters that improved the view to the rear of the aircraft.

The Mosquito B Mk IX could carry four 500 pound bombs in the bomb bay and a pair of 500 pound bombs on universal carriers mounted on the wing in place of the standard underwing fuel tanks. This gave the standard B Mk IX a total bomb load of 3,000 pounds.

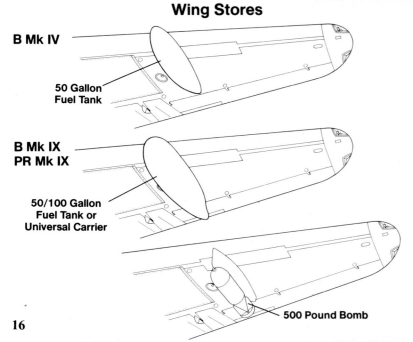

Numerous Mosquitoes chalked up more than 100 sorties and this PR Mk IX (ML897) "D for Dorothy' of No 1409 Meteorological Flight proudly displayed its score on the nose (161). The unit flew weather reconnaissance over Europe, providing reliable weather forecasting services for Bomber Command.

This overall PRU Blue Mosquito PR MK IX (MM230) carries two fifty gallon drop tanks under the wings. One of de Havilland's goals throughout the war was to find ways to increase the range of the PR variants so that they could cover any target in Europe from bases in the UK and Italy.

This Mosquito B Mk IX (LR503/GB-F) of No 105 Squadron completed 213 operational sorties as part of the Path Finder Force. The aircraft carried its full scoreboard and personal insignia on 23 March 1945, just two months before it was totally destroyed in a fatal crash in Canada.

Photo reconnaissance Mosquitoes usually carried an overall PRU Blue camouflage finish. This PR Mk IX (LR412) carries a small A just forward of the fuselage roundel as its individual aircraft identification letter. (IWM)

Mosquito B Mk XVI

The Mosquito B Mk XVI was a pressurized development of the B Mk IX which gave the aircraft an operational ceiling of some 35,000 feet. The aircraft was equipped with the full range of electronic detection/counter-measures devices available to Bomber Command in the latter half of the war and represented the peak of wartime Mosquito development in the high speed bomber program.

The prototype B Mk XVI was a converted B Mk IV (DZ540) fitted with 1,680 hp Merlin 72 engines. The prototype Mk XVI first flew in July of 1943 and deliveries of production aircraft commenced that December when No 109 Squadron was equipped with the aircraft. The first twelve aircraft off the assembly line were configured with conventional bomb bay doors and carried the standard bomb load of four 500 pound bombs internally and two under wing. With the thirteenth aircraft, production (which totalled 402 aircraft) shifted to the bulged bomb bay doors allowing the B Mk XVI to carrying the 4,000 pound "Cookie" bomb. Additionally, the Avro company had developed a special bomb carrier capable of holding six 500 pound bombs, which could be carried by the B Mk XVI in place of the 4,000 pound bomb.

For target marking, the majority of B XVIs were equipped with Gee-H and H2S radar, usually carried in the nose behind the glass nose. A few examples had the radar antenna mounted in a ventral radome not unlike their four-engined heavy bomber counterparts. Various detection and protective electronic systems were fitted, depending on the mission, including Album Leaf, Boozer, Fishpond and Monica.

The Mosquito B Mk XVI was the most important wartime Mosquito bomber variant, serving with eight squadrons in the Light Night Striking Forces, including: Nos 139, 105, 109, 692, 128, 571 and 608 Squadrons. Between January and May of 1945, the LNSF Mosquito squadrons dropped a total of 2,959 4,000 pound "Cookies" on German targets.

Ground crewmen move a 4,000 pound "Cookie" bomb into position for loading into a Mosquito B Mk XVI of No 128 Squadron. The bomb's message reveals the ground crewmen's typical irreverence toward the enemy. This Cookie was dropped on a German target during the Christmas 1944 period.

The Royal Navy was also among the operators of the B Mk XVI. The service took four examples on charge under the designation Met Mk XVI. These aircraft were used in the weather reconnaissance role.

Mosquito PR Mk XVI

The PR Mk XVI entered service during December of 1943 with Nos 140 and 400 Squadrons. The aircraft was basically a B Mk XVI modified with a three camera installation, additional internal fuel (bomb bay tanks) and a modified canopy. The canopy was modified with top and rear blisters which improved rear view for the navigator and ended the tendency of the standard canopy to ice up at high altitudes.

Fuselage Development

Mosquito B Mk IV

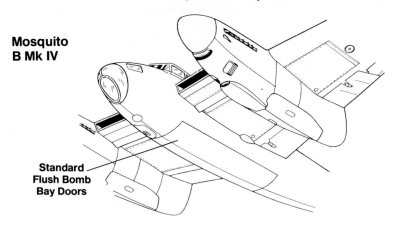

Standard Flush Bomb Bay Doors

Mosquito B Mk XVI

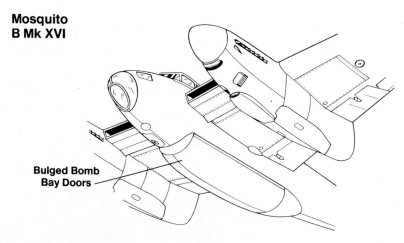

Bulged Bomb Bay Doors

A number of PR Mk XVIs were delivered to the 8th Air Force, USAAF during February of 1944. These aircraft were used for the weather reconnaissance and photographic roles by the 25th Bombardment Group at Watton and for experimental work involving the H2X radar (the American version of the H2S radar). Six Mosquitoes were modified with the radar and flown by the 482nd Bomb Group.

No 140 Squadron was the first to use the PR XVI operationally, followed by No 540 Squadron. One of the Mosquitoes of No 540 Squadron was able to satisfy an urgent need for photos of Berlin during a mission on 19 February, even though German fighters were sighted at altitudes up to 42,000 feet and they were pursued off the target by flak bursts. Fitted with 100 gallon drop tanks, Mosquito PR Mk XVIs were flying missions of over 2,000 miles, including missions over Norway. Another mission flown by stripped down PR Mk XVIs was Operation HAYCOCK, a daily air mail service between England and Cairo in connection with the Yalta Conference. A similar service was performed by Mosquitoes of No 544 Squadron during the later Potsdam Conference.

A ground crewman waves off three night flying Mosquitoes B Mk XVIs taxi out to begin another night's work. The aircraft were all assigned to No 128 Squadron based at Wyton. At one point the squadron flew thirteen successive night missions against Berlin.

Armorers manhandle a 4,000 pound "Cookie" into position under the fuselage of a Mosquito B Mk XVI (PF432) coded H5-W of No 128 Squadron at Wyton on 21 March 1945. To carry the large 4,000 pound bomb the bomb bay door were bulged, giving the Mosquito a somewhat "pot bellied" look.

The flight crew entry for Mosquito bomber variants was through a hatch under the nose section. Fighter-bomber and night fighter Mosquitoes has a door on the starboard side of the fuselage. The pilot of this Mosquito of No 128 Squadron boards the bomber while the navigator waits holding his large canvas "nav bag."

A number of Mosquitoes were paid for by public subscriptions. Funds raised by Britons and foreign nationals living abroad were used to buy aircraft for the RAF and usually these aircraft carried special markings. This B Mk XVI carried the inscription *LISBON BRITISH* in the nose in White.

A Mosquito B XVI shares a dispersal at Wahn, Germany, with a gun armed T III. trainer. The B Mk XVI (PF553/C) was assigned to No 14 Squadron, while the T III carried the "UP" identification code of No 605 Squadron. The last aircraft in line is a Wellington Mk X. (RAF Museum)

The installation of radar antennas altered the Mosquito's nose contours in various ways. This Mosquito B Mk XVI carried a American built H2X radar set, equivalent to the British H2S, in a large bulbous radome. Several Mosquito PR Mk XVIs configured in this manner saw service with the U.S. 8th Air Force.

This Mosquito PR XVI (NS534) on the ramp at an Operational Conversion Unit (OCU) in the Middle East carried full D-Day Black and White invasion stripes even though the aircraft was thousands of miles from the Normandy beaches. (Frank Marshall)

Fuselage Development

B Mk XVI

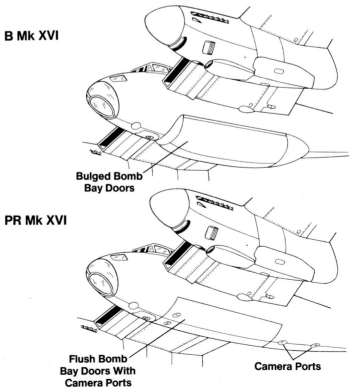

This PR Mk XVI was one of the Mosquitoes on the ramp at the de Havilland Hatfield plant on 2 February 1944. At this time, de Havilland was turning out some twenty-five Mosquitoes a day. The two aircraft immediately behind the PR Mk XVI are gun nosed FB Mk VI fighter-bombers.

Bulged Bomb Bay Doors

PR Mk XVI

Flush Bomb Bay Doors With Camera Ports

Camera Ports

PR Mosquitoes carrying the Black and White D-Day invasion stripes had the underwing slipper tanks painted Black so they would not contrast with the invasion markings. This PR Mk XVI (NS502) of No 544 Squadron carried its individual identification letter M under its serial number in Black against the last White invasion stripe. (Harry Holmes)

This PR XVI (NS688) was one of several Mosquitoes that broke speed records during their delivery flights to India. Flight Lieutenant Linton and Warrant Officer Gaudie flew to Karachi in 16 hours and 46 minutes on 4/5 November 1944. The aircraft carried the marking SNAKE on the fuselage indicating it was "reserved for South East Asia Command."

In high demand in all theaters, PR Mosquito became a common and very welcome sight around the world. No 2 Photographic Reconnaissance Unit was renumbered as No 680 Squadron in February of 1943 and equipped with Mosquito PR XVIs the following year at Foggia, Italy. These PR Mk XVIs had Red and White tail stripes and Yellow spinners as a recognition aid.

Canopy Development

B Mk XVI

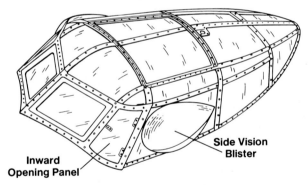

Inward Opening Panel

Side Vision Blister

Mosquito PR XVIs (NS644/G) carry the Red and White recognition stripes of No 680 Squadron. These aircraft, often flown by crews of No 60 Squadron South African Air Force, carried the markings to prevent Allied fighter pilots from mistaking them for Luftwaffe Me 210s.

Navigator's Blister

PR Mk XVI

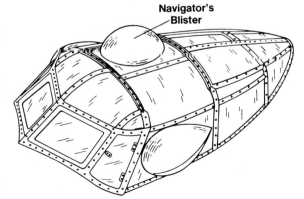

An overall PRU Blue Mosquito PR XVI undergoes servicing on the ramp at Bengal, India during March of 1945. The aircraft in the background carries an overall Silver dope finish with Black South East Asia Command recognition bands on the fin, tailplane and wings. (Aeroplane)

A number of Mosquitoes were modified to carry the bomber navigation H2S radar in a bulbous ventral radome. This B Mk XVI (ML926/G) was used to conduct a series of flight tests of the radar installation from Defford airfield. This installation did not become a standard feature.

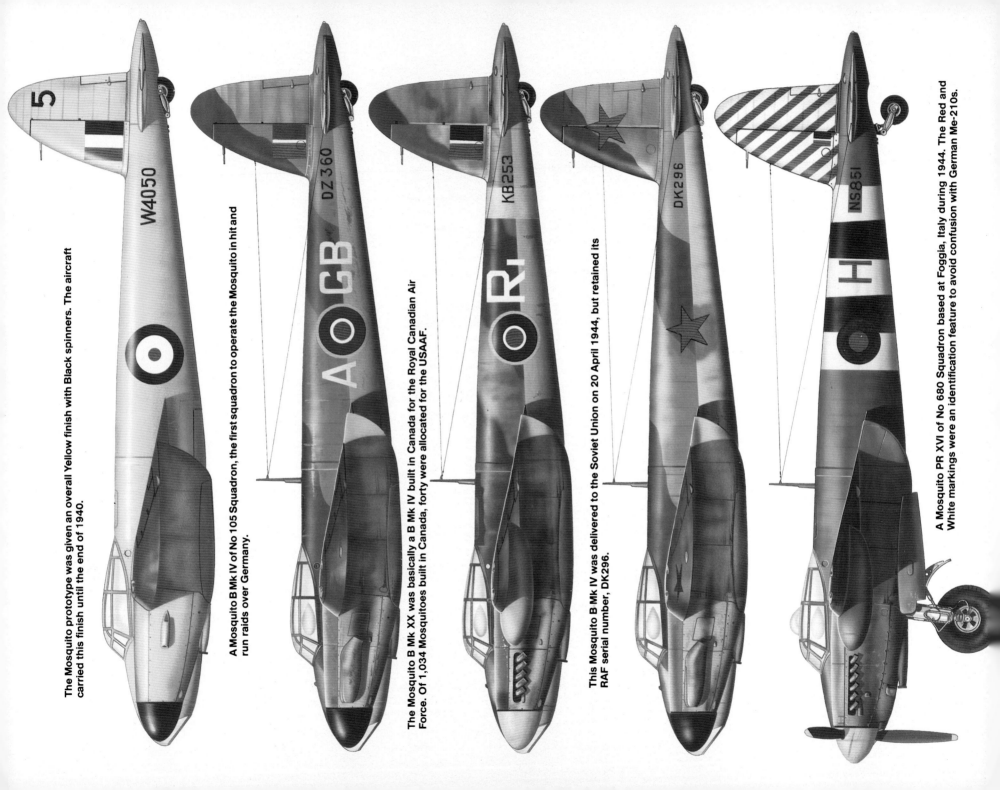

The Mosquito prototype was given an overall Yellow finish with Black spinners. The aircraft carried this finish until the end of 1940.

A Mosquito B Mk IV of No 105 Squadron, the first squadron to operate the Mosquito in hit and run raids over Germany.

The Mosquito B Mk XX was basically a B Mk IV built in Canada for the Royal Canadian Air Force. Of 1,034 Mosquitoes built in Canada, forty were allocated for the USAAF.

This Mosquito B Mk IV was delivered to the Soviet Union on 20 April 1944, but retained its RAF serial number, DK296.

A Mosquito PR XVI of No 680 Squadron based at Foggia, Italy during 1944. The Red and White markings were an identification feature to avoid confusion with German Me-210s.

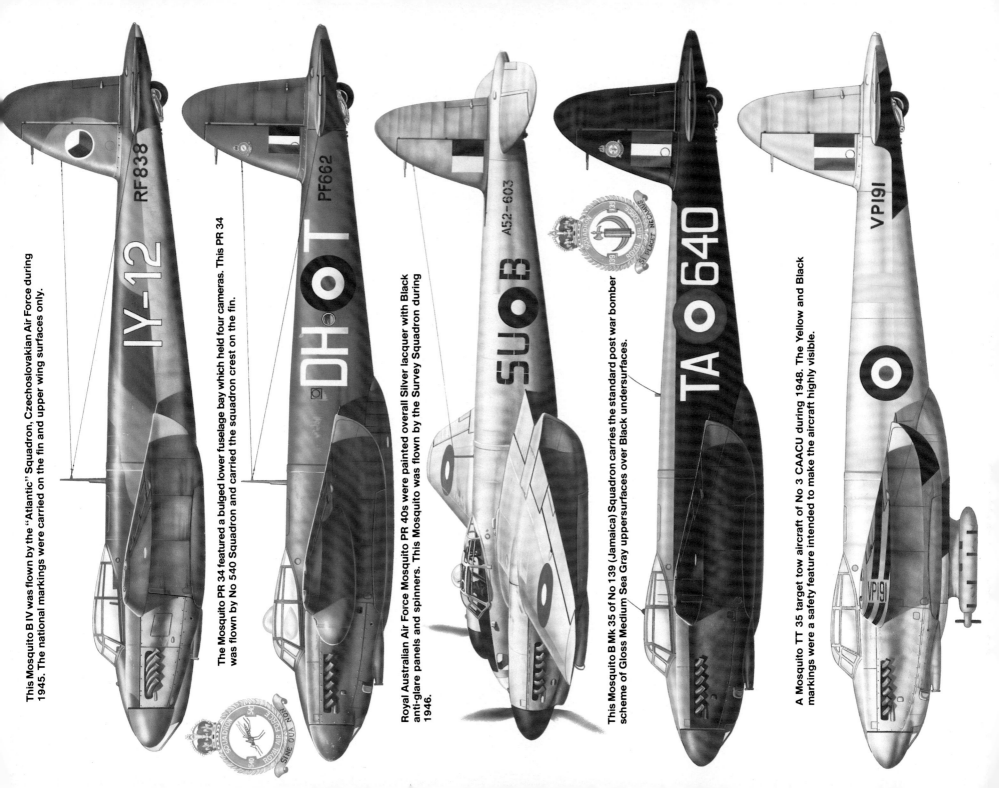

This Mosquito B IV was flown by the "Atlantic" Squadron, Czechoslovakian Air Force during 1945. The national markings were carried on the fin and upper wing surfaces only.

The Mosquito PR 34 featured a bulged lower fuselage bay which held four cameras. This PR 34 was flown by No 540 Squadron and carried the squadron crest on the fin.

Royal Australian Air Force Mosquito PR 40s were painted overall Silver lacquer with Black anti-glare panels and spinners. This Mosquito was flown by the Survey Squadron during 1946.

This Mosquito B Mk 35 of No 139 (Jamaica) Squadron carries the standard post war bomber scheme of Gloss Medium Sea Gray uppersurfaces over Black undersurfaces.

A Mosquito TT 35 target tow aircraft of No 3 CAACU during 1948. The Yellow and Black markings were a safety feature intended to make the aircraft highly visible.

Mosquito B Mk XX

The Mosquito B Mk XX had the distinction of being the last of the Mosquito variants to be officially identified with Roman numerals. The B Mk XX was a Canadian built variant of the Mosquito B Mk IV that incorporated equipment from both Canadian and U.S. production sources. All these aircraft were powered by Packard-built Merlin engines. The first eighty aircraft off the production line had 1,460 hp Packard Merlin 31s and the balance of the production run (245 aircraft) were powered by 1,460 hp Packard Merlin 33s.

By the end of 1942 at least four B Mk XXs were completed and ready for shipment to England. It was decided to send these aircraft across the Atlantic by air and during August of 1943 the first two Mosquito B Mk XXs were ferried to England. One aircraft was flown by American contract civil aircrews (KN162) while the second aircraft was flown by an RAF crew. These aircraft were equipped with 200 gallon bomb bay tanks and arrived in England on 12 August after staging through Greenland, Iceland and Scotland. Once in England, the aircraft were tested and accepted, although the solid windscreen was replaced by a British Triplex sandwich windscreen.

As Canadian aircraft began to arrive in greater numbers, No 13 Maintenance Unit at RAF Henlow was chosen to be the receipt point for all Canadian built Mosquitoes being ferried across the Atlantic. All non-common spare parts for the B Mk XXs were stored at this location, which was picked for its proximity to bases where RCAF Mosquito units were being formed.

No 139 Squadron, RAF was the first combat unit to equip with the B Mk XX, with their initial sorties being made on 2 December 1943. No 627 followed, with the unit flying its first operations with the new variant on 7 July 1944. Both Nos 139 and 162 Squadrons had a number of B Mk XXs on strength fitted with H2S radar, the antenna for the radar being housed behind an opaque nose cap. Four Light Night Striking Force units, Nos 128, 142, 163 and 608 Squadrons, also flew the B Mk XX.

The USAAF took delivery of thirty-four aircraft that had been converted to the F-8 photo reconnaissance configuration, although these were not as widely used as the Mosquito PR Mk XVIs delivered earlier from British production.

This Canadian-built Mosquito B Mk XX (KB326) was named *ACTON ONTARIO CANADA* and was the first of two Canadian built aircraft that arrived at Hatfield on 12 August 1943. The B Mk XX was basically a DHC built B Mk IV.

This Canadian B Mk XX suffered a failed port landing gear on landing. The condition of the port propeller indicates that the engine was still running when the crash occurred. The fuselage markings identify this Mosquito as being assigned to a training unit in Canada. (RCAF)

Crashes, or "prangs" in British slang, were a fact of life on training bases, and the RCAF had its share. This Mosquito B Mk XX has had the starboard wingtip wrecked when the aircraft ground looped. In addition to the failed starboard landing gear, the bent up propeller indicates the engine was running at the time of impact and was probably ruined. (Aeroplane)

Mosquito B Mk 25

When Mosquito mark numbers reached XX (20), it was decided that, to avoid confusion, Arabic numbers would be adopted for all future Mosquito variants. During the later half of the Mosquito's production life, a number of new models appeared, although most of these were conversions of earlier marks and were similar to models already in service.

The Mosquito B Mk 25 was one of these. The B Mk 25 was a Canadian built variant of the de Havilland of Canada Ltd. Mosquito Mk XX powered by two-stage supercharged 1,620 hp Packard-built Merlin 225 engines. These engines enabled the B Mk 25 to carry bomb loads of up to 4,000 pounds. Royal Canadian Air Force units received thirty-eight aircraft, while the majority of the production run (343 aircraft) went to the RAF and Royal Navy (70 aircraft). At least five of these aircraft (KB409, KB416, KB490, KB561 and KB625) were locally modified by RAF units with bulged bomb bay doors to accept 4,000 pound "Cookie" bombs.

B Mk 25s were used by Nos 139, 162, 163 and 608 Squadrons and with No 614 Squadron in the Middle East, which was working up on the aircraft in the pathfinder role when the war ended.

After the war a number of Mosquito B Mk 25s were sold in the United States. One aircraft, registered N66313, took part in the 1948 Bendix Trophy Race carrying race number 81. The aircraft was sponsored by Capitol Airways and was flown by the airline's president, Jesse Stallings. The Mosquito placed fifth at an average speed of 341.1 mph. Another Mosquito B Mk 25, registered N37878 and named *The Wooden Wonder*, took part in the 1949 race, placing fourth overall at an average speed of 343.575 mph. This aircraft carried extra fuel in the bomb bay and had fifty gallon slipper tanks under the wings. The transparent nose cap was replaced for the race with a smooth fairing to streamline the aircraft.

Several other Mosquito B Mk 25s were used in speed record attempts. One was used in an around-the-world speed record attempt. The Mosquito, registered N1203V, left California flying east and reached Karachi, India before engine trouble forced an end to the attempt.

The Mosquito B Mk 25 was a Canadian built B Mk XX fitted with improved two-stage Packard-built Merlin 225 engines. Many were later converted with bulged bomb bay doors to carry a 4,000 pound bomb. A total of 400 aircraft were built. (Aeroplane)

Mosquito PR Mk 34

The Mosquito PR Mk 34 was a progressive development of the earlier PR Mk XVI intended for use in the Far East theater of operations. The aircraft was powered by 1,635 hp Merlin 25 engines and differed from the earlier PR Mk XVI in having bulged bomb bay doors. This allowed the PR Mk 34 to carry additional fuel tanks in the bomb bay giving the aircraft a total internal fuel of 792 gallons. The underwing fuel tanks had double the capacity (200 gallons) of the tanks used on the XVI, giving the Mk 34 a total fuel load of 1,192 gallons and a range of some 3,340 miles. The aircraft also had a pressurized cabin for operations at high altitudes.

The camera installation consisted of two F52 split vertical cameras mounted in front of the fuselage fuel tanks, two F52s vertical cameras and one F24 oblique camera mounted to the rear of the tank. The F24 could be replaced by a K17 for survey work.

Just prior to VJ Day, No 684 Squadron deployed a detachment of PR Mk 34s to the Cocos Islands arriving in June of 1945. From this location the detachment began flying sorties over Malaya, Singapore and the Dutch East Indies, with the first mission being flown on 3 July 1945. By the end of August, seven aircraft had arrived and by the time Japan surrendered, the unit had flown some thirty-eight sorties, photographing Kuala Lumpur, Malacca, Sumatra, Java, Singapore, Palembang and other important targets.

In June of 1948, a state of emergency was declared in Malaya as a result of growing communist terrorism and attacks on British citizens. As a result, the RAF began anti-terrorist operations under the code name, Operation FIREDOG. Photo reconnaissance missions were flown over the area by Mosquito PR Mk 34s (and Spitfire PR Mk 19s) of No 81 Squadron based at Tengah on Singapore Island. Over the course of the Malaya campaign, the squadron flew some 4,000 sorties, photographing 34,000 square miles of territory. Additionally, the unit flew anti-piracy patrols over the waters surrounding Malaya and Borneo. The squadron had the honor of flying the last operational Mosquito mission flown by an active RAF unit. On 15 December 1955 a Mosquito PR 34, flown by Flying Officer Knox photographed two terrorist camps and when he landed, the aircraft was officially retired (being replaced by Meteor PR Mk 10s).

In England, the PR Mk 34 was also used in a number of research projects. One such project was undertaken by the Gust Research Unit which used PR Mk 34s to investigate clear air turbulence. No 540 Squadron used PR Mk 34s to photograph the effects of floods that hit England's east coast during 1953. The unit flew some 40,000 miles within six days, producing some 16,500 negatives and some 100,000 prints, enabling officials to quickly direct rescue and repair efforts where they were needed most.

Several PR Mk 34s were sold to civil operators and converted for aerial mapping. These aircraft were modified with a dorsal D/F loop antenna and radio navigational aid antennas under each wingtip. At least six were operated by a company flying survey work over Libya in connection with oil exploration during 1957.

A total of 181 aircraft were built, fifty of which were completed by Percival Aircraft. Later thirty-five aircraft were converted to the PR Mk 34A standard, which involved fitting the aircraft with 1,710 hp Merlin 24 engines.

This overall PRU Blue PR Mk 34 (VL618) has had its starboard flap replaced by one taken from a Mosquito painted a different color. The circular windows in the bomb bay doors are camera ports for vertical and oblique cameras, while the three smaller ports under the rear fuselage are recognition lights.

The blister on the canopy was used by the navigator for sun shots and to keep watch for enemy fighters trying to intercept the Mosquito. This PR Mk 34 is overall PRU Blue with Blue and Red roundels on the fuselage and upper wing. No roundels were carried on the lower wings.

A Mosquito PR Mk 34 (RG241/K) at Saint Eval after a long range flight. While most Mosquitoes were a delight to fly, the Mk 34 was not as highly rated. Pilots felt that the aircraft was too heavy, with a stiff elevator control and an occasional reluctance to leave the ground. (W. Gill)

Camera Installation

PR Mk XVI

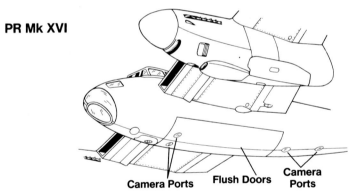

Camera Ports   Flush Doors   Camera Ports

PR Mk 34

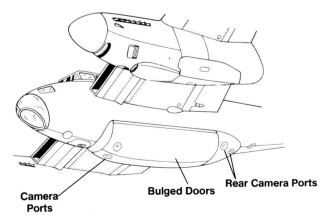

Camera Ports   Bulged Doors   Rear Camera Ports

This Mosquito PR Mk 34 (RG176) is fitted with 200 gallon underwing slipper fuel tanks, the largest capacity tanks carried by the Mosquito. The underwing slipper tanks came in three basic sizes: 50 gallon, 100 gallon and 200 gallon.

Ground crews prepare this Mosquito PR Mk 34 of No 22 Squadron for the next stage of a long range, ferry flight between Egypt and Singapore. The Mosquito was serving as the navigation ship for a squadron of Vampire jet fighters deploying to Singapore. (J Stewart)

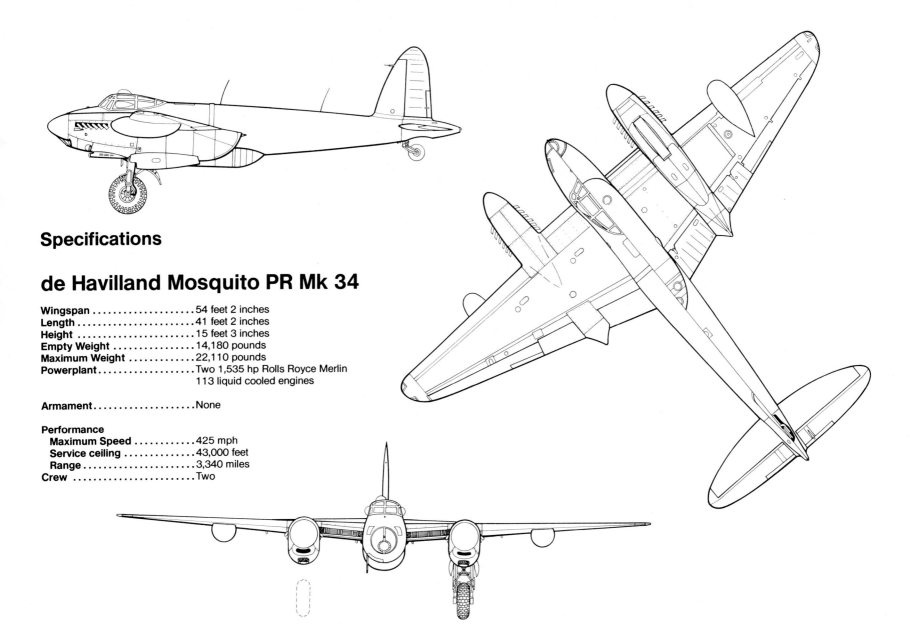

Specifications

de Havilland Mosquito PR Mk 34

Wingspan .54 feet 2 inches
Length . . . . .41 feet 2 inches
Height . . . . .15 feet 3 inches
Empty Weight . . . . .14,180 pounds
Maximum Weight . . . . .22,110 pounds
Powerplant . . . . .Two 1,535 hp Rolls Royce Merlin
113 liquid cooled engines

Armament .None

Performance
  Maximum Speed . . . . .425 mph
  Service ceiling . . . . .43,000 feet
  Range . . . . .3,340 miles
Crew . . . . .Two

This overall Silver dope Mosquito PR Mk 34 (RG314) of No 81 Squadron was the last operational Mosquito in the RAF. At the time, No 81 Squadron was involved in Operation FIREDOG, the air campaign against communist terrorists in Malaya. (Thetford)

During 1948 the operational strength of the RAF Benson Photo Recon Flight included this Mosquito PR Mk 34 (RG190/6C-E) and the Spitfire PR Mk XIX (6C-W). It was not uncommon for PR units to operate more than one aircraft type. As a result, missions could be scheduled taking advantage of the best features of the various aircraft.

Flying Officer Brown pre-flights this Mosquito PR Mk 34 (RG314) of No 81 Squadron based at Seletar, Singapore, shortly before the aircraft was officially retired. The aircraft made the last operational sortie by an RAF Mosquito on 15 December 1955. The flight was a photo run over a terrorist target in Malaya.

Mosquito PR Mk 34s of No 772 Squadron, Fleet Air Arm at RNAS Abroath, Scotland carries an overall Azure Blue camouflage finish with "B" type roundels and Black serials. The unit was at the Scottish base from 7 January to 31 October 1948. (Dave Howley)

Mosquito B Mk 35

The Mosquito B Mk 35 was the last bomber variant produced. The prototype made its first flight on 12 March 1945 and deliveries of production aircraft were beginning just as the war ended. A total of 274 aircraft were built, including sixty-five by Airspeed.

The aircraft was very similar to the earlier B Mk XVI and featured bulged bomb bay doors for carrying 4,000 pound bombs and a pressurized cabin. The B Mk 35 was powered by the 1,710 hp Merlin 114 engine giving it a top speed of 415 mph at 42,000 feet. Additionally, the B Mk 35 carried four to six wingtip mounted dipole antennas used for the "Gee-H" bombing/navigational aid.

The B Mk 35 first entered service with Nos 109 and 139 Squadrons of the Pathfinder Force based at Hemswell. These two units were the sole Bomber Command squadrons to re-equip with the B Mk 35. Three squadrons of the British Air Forces of Occupation (BAFO) in Germany re-equipped with the B Mk 35: Nos 69, 14 and 98 Squadrons.

In July of 1952, No 109 Squadron finally retired its Mosquitoes in favor of the Canberra, being followed by No 139 Squadron in June of 1953. The squadrons in Germany replaced their Mosquitoes with Vampire jet fighter-bombers. As the B Mk 35s were phased out of first line service they were used for a number of secondary roles. One was used by the Empire Test Pilots School, this aircraft being modified with a smoke system for display flying. Another aircraft was used by de Havilland Propellers Ltd. during the mid-1950s for testing new propeller designs.

Ten aircraft were later converted to the photo reconnaissance role as PR Mk 35s. These aircraft were modified by de Havilland at Leavesden and four were taken on strength by B Flight of No 58 Squadron.

Some 105 B Mk 35s were converted by Brooklands Aviation Ltd. for the target towing mission under the designation TT Mk 35s. Four drogue targets were carried in the bomb bay. These were towed behind the aircraft at the end of a 6,000 foot steel cable. The cable was reeled in and out by an ML Type G wind driven winch which was mounted in a cylindrical fairing carried under the fuselage, just behind the crew entry door, although problems with the winch led to it being removed from most TT 35s. The aircraft that deleted the winch used banner targets in place of the drogue targets. The banners were released through holes in the bomb bay doors, with a total of two banners being carried in the bomb bay.

The Mosquito TT Mk 35 served with a number of RAF target towing flights throughout the 1950s. By 1 October of 1957 only one remained, being based at RAF Schleswigland, Germany. This unit had eight TT Mk 35s and towed targets for NATO anti-aircraft gunners over the gunnery ranges at Todenhorf. The TT Mk 35 was also assigned to No 229 Operational Conversion Unit to provide transition training for pilots of Nos 1 and 3 Civilian Anti-Aircraft Co-operation Units (CAACU). These units were manned by civil pilots under contract to the Air Ministry. The contractor supplied the pilots and ground crews, while the RAF supplied the aircraft. No 3 CAACU was based at Exeter and provided target services for Navy and Army units in southern England. The Mosquito could fly missions of up to four and a half hours.

During 1963, three TT Mk 35s were sold to Mirisch Films Ltd. for use in the movie "633 Squadron." The aircraft were modified to resemble FB Mk IV fighter-bombers with dummy guns in the overpainted nose section and accurate wartime camouflage schemes. The filming was done in Scotland and after completion one of the surviving aircraft was sold to the Confederate Air Force in the United States, joining another TT Mk 35 that had been presented to the Smithsonian Institute.

Technicians check the engine mounts of this B Mk 35 on the Airspeed production line. Airspeed took part in the Mosquito production program and began production of some 300 aircraft in April of 1945. The contracts were all for Mosquito B VI and B Mk 35s, with the majority of the aircraft being completed after the war. The aircraft in the background are Airspeed Oxford trainers.

The Mosquito in the foreground is a B Mk 35 (VR794), the last Mosquito bomber production variant. The aircraft were at the Airspeed Portsmouth plant for overhaul during 1947. Later, VR794 was sold to Spartan Air Services and registered CF-HMk.

Ten TT Mk 35s were sold to Spartan Air Services Ltd. of Ottawa, Canada for air survey work. The aircraft were modified by Derby Aviation with a new clear (unframed) transparent nose section and three camera windows were installed in the fuselage underside (forward and to the rear of the bomb bay). The aircraft were equipped with Swiss made RC-5 aerial mapping cameras. A sixty-five gallon fuel tank was installed in the bomb bay area and the bomb bay doors were replaced by a wooden panel to reduce weight, and a DF loop antenna was installed on the fuselage spine. To operate the photographic systems a third crew member was carried. The aircraft were given Canadian civil registrations and were used to fly mapping missions throughout North and South America and in Kenya. One of the ex-Spartan aircraft was reportedly later restored in Canada by the Royal Canadian Air Cadets.

A number of TT Mk 35s were also used for the weather reconnaissance role during 1956 under the designation Met Mk 35.

Clustered around the Hemswell tower, Mosquito B Mk 35s of No 139 (Jamaica) Squadron undergo routine maintenance before another sortie. With a fine war record, the squadron had flown Mosquitoes for some eleven years when these B Mk 35s were replaced by Canberras during 1953.

Mosquito B Mk 35s of No 139 (Jamaica) Squadron line up on the runway at Hemswell during May of 1950. The overall Silver dope aircraft carry Black code letters, while the Silver and Black aircraft have White codes; all three aircraft have Red spinners. (Aeroplane)

Antenna Configuration

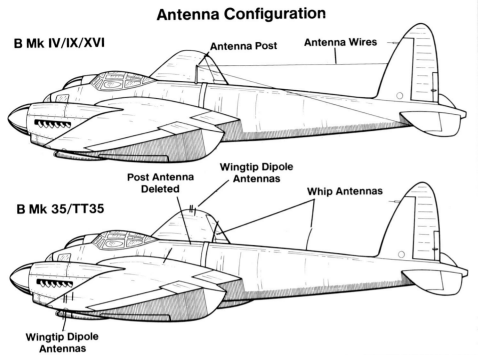

B Mk IV/IX/XVI

Antenna Post
Antenna Wires

B Mk 35/TT35

Post Antenna Deleted
Wingtip Dipole Antennas
Whip Antennas
Wingtip Dipole Antennas

The pod under the fuselage of this Mosquito TT Mk 35 (RS719) is an air driven winch. Problems were encountered with this winch and most TT Mk 35s did not carry it. The aircraft had Black and Yellow diagonal stripes under the wings. (Robertson)

This Mosquito TT Mk 35 (TR610/Y) was believed to have been on strength with the Gibraltar Target Towing flight during 1954. The aircraft provided target services for Royal Navy units in the Mediterranean area. (Howley)

An overall Silver dope Mosquito TT Mk 35 (TA634/53) target tow aircraft is refueled outside a hangar at Exeter, Devon on 15 August 1960. The band around the fuselage is Yellow. (Holmes)

This Mosquito TT Mk 35 (VP141/54) of No 3 Civilian Anti-Aircraft Cooperation Unit (CAACU) based at Exeter, was flown by the unit's chief pilot Harry Ellis. The stripes on the wings and rear fuselage were Day-Glo Orange. (Aeroplane)

The Mosquito TT Mk 35 carried the serial under the wings in large Black letters in addition to the Yellow and Black recognition stripes. The device on the fuselage underside just in front of the roundel is a metal framework designed to keep the drogue cable from hitting the tailplane.

Among the postwar civilian users of surplus Mosquito B Mk 35s was Spartan Air Services of Ottawa, Canada. The company used ten B Mk 35s for photographic survey work. The aircraft were converted to the PR role by Derby Aviation Ltd. in the UK.

This B Mk 35 was registered in the U.S., then seemingly abandoned at North Hollywood Airport, California during 1958. The aircraft, N9909F, had been previously registered in New Zealand as ZK-BCV.

Mosquito TT Mk 39

General Aircraft Ltd. converted a total of twenty-four Mosquito B Mk XVI bombers to the target tow configuration under specification Q.19/45. These aircraft were intended to replace the Miles Monitor TT Mk 2 in Royal Navy service and received the designation Mosquito TT Mk 39.

The TT Mk 39 was the most unusual Mosquito variant ever flown. The aircraft featured a new forward fuselage, which increased the overall length to 43 feet 4 inches. The aircraft was fitted with an enlarged glazed nose to accommodate a camera operator's position. The camera operator was to record the intended miss distance of gunfire from fighters attacking a towed target drogue. A second extra crewman, who operated the drogue winch, was housed in a dorsal turret-like fairing midway on the upper fuselage.

Drogue targets were streamed from a winch housed in the bomb bay, which was powered by a retractable wind-driven generator that was housed in the forward portion of the bomb bay. For exercises, "Window" anti-radar foil strips could be dropped from an opening panel in the nose section. For ferry flights, the nose section could be removed and replaced by a solid nose that resembled the radar nose of an NF Mk 38 night-fighter.

Two prototype TT Mk 39s were built along with twenty-two production aircraft. These aircraft served with UK based Fleet Requirements Units (FRUs) and with No 728 FRU on Malta during 1948-50. Along with their target towing duties, the TT Mk 39 was used for radar calibration flights.

The TT Mk 39 could tow a thirty-two foot span target at 279 mph and a sixteen foot target at 292 mph.

One of the most unusual Mosquito modifications was the large transparent nose of the TT Mk 39 target tug. This wooden mock-up was used to finalize the shape of the nose section that was installed on a Mosquito Mk XVI. The new nose housed a crewman who photographed intercepts of towed target drogues.

This operational Mosquito TT Mk 39 (PF576) carries Black and Yellow stripes under the wings. The air driven winch for the target drogue was retractable and was lowered from the bomb bay when needed. (Aeroplane)

This aircraft served as the aerodynamic prototype for the Royal Navy's Mosquito TT Mk 39 target tug conversion program and was configured with a mock-up of the extended nose section and the dorsal cupola that housed the drogue operator's position.

Sea Mosquito TR Mk 33

The Sea Mosquito (TR Mk 33) evolved from a Royal Navy requirement for a carrier based, twin engined, torpedo bomber/reconnaissance/strike aircraft. In response, de Havilland modified a Mosquito FB IV fighter-bomber as a test-bed to evaluate the "navalized" Mosquito. The aircraft was modified with an arrestor hook, and the fuselage was reinforced for deck landings. A total of two prototypes were converted (LR359 and LR307) during 1944 and these were followed by two additional aircraft that were used mainly for handling trials and weapons testing.

Production Sea Mosquitoes were given the designation TR Mk 33 identifying the role as a Torpedo bomber/Reconnaissance aircraft. The TR Mk 33 was powered by 1,635 hp Merlin 25 engines driving four blade propellers instead of the three blade units used by earlier Mosquito variants. The aircraft was fitted with folding wings and the landing gear was changed. The rubber block compression shock absorbing landing gear proved to be too stiff for deck landings and it was replaced by an oleo-pneumatic type landing gear.

The Sea Mosquito was armed with four internally mounted 20MM cannons (in the forward portion of the bomb bay) and two 500 pound bombs in the rear portion of the bomb bay. The main armament was an 18 inch Mk XV or XVII naval torpedo which was carried on the aircraft centerline. Alternatively, a 2,000 bomb or mine could be carried in place of the torpedo. Like earlier Mosquito variants, the Sea Mosquito could also carry underwing drop tank or bombs.

The Sea Mosquito had a solid nose with thimble type radome for an ASH radar. To assist with high gross weight operations, the aircraft was fitted with Rocket Assisted Take Off Gear (RATOG) which consisted of two RATO bottles on each side of the lower rear fuselage.

Deck landing trials were successfully carried out aboard HMS INDEFATIGABLE by the prototypes during 1944; however, the Sea Mosquito never actually served as a carrier based aircraft. The first operational Sea Mosquito squadron was No 811 Squadron,

which received its first TR Mk 33 in August of 1946. The operational life of the Sea Mosquito was short, with the squadron being disbanded in July of 1947. After that time, the Sea Mosquito served mainly with Fleet Requirements Units such as Nos 771, 772 762, 778 and 790 Squadrons in the United Kingdom.

A total of fifty Sea Mosquito TR 33 were built, and some fourteen of these were later overhauled and sold to the Israeli Air Force during 1954-55. During the overhaul the arrestor hook, catapult gear and other items of naval equipment were deleted.

Sea Mosquito TR Mk 37

The TR Mk 33 was superseded in service by the TR Mk 37 which differed from the earlier aircraft only in the nose radome. The TR Mk 37 carried a larger, longer thimble radome to house a British built ASV Mk III radar in place of the American built ASH radar used on the TR Mk 33. A total of fourteen (serialed VT724-VT737) were built and these aircraft served briefly with No 703 Squadron, before being relegated to second line duties.

This strengthened and modified Mosquito FB Mk VI (LR359) made the first Mosquito carrier landing aboard HMS INDEFATIGABLE on 25 March 1944 to prove the concept of operating heavy twin-engined aircraft from Royal Navy carriers.

This Mosquito (LR359) served as the prototype for the Sea Mosquito TR Mk 33. the aircraft was modified with a strengthened fuselage, arrestor hook, oleo-pneumatic landing gear and four blade propellers.

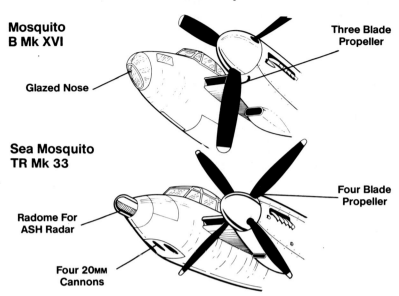

Sea Mosquito

Mosquito B Mk XVI

Glazed Nose

Three Blade Propeller

Sea Mosquito TR Mk 33

Radome For ASH Radar

Four 20MM Cannons

Four Blade Propeller

One of the two Sea Mosquito TR Mk 33 prototype that were used during the test program for weapons trials. The shackles and sway braces for the centerline torpedo are visible under the forward fuselage just behind the gun ports for the four internal 20MM cannons.

The Sea Mosquito Mk 33 featured folding wings to allow it to be stored in the hangar bays of Royal Navy carriers. The aircraft never actually served aboard ship, since it arrived too late and the Royal Navy had a far superior aircraft in development — the de Havilland Sea Hornet.

The cockpit of a Royal Navy Mosquito T33 was dominated by the radar scope of the American developed ASH search radar on the right and the reflector gunsight (center). The gunsight has a substantial crash pad mounted in front of the sight.

The Navy decided that the de Havilland Sea Hornet would serve aboard its carriers and the Sea Mosquitoes served in shore based units and stations. This TR Mk 33 (TW256/593) was assigned to No 771 Sqn based at Lee-on-Solent during the early 1950s.

The Sea Mosquito TT Mk 37 was the follow-on torpedo reconnaissance aircraft to the Sea Mosquito TT Mk 33. The aircraft featured a much larger tapered nose radome that housed a British-built ASV Mk XIII radar in place of the American ASH radar used on the TT Mk 33.

Foreign Operators

Some fourteen nations used the Mosquito in one form or another. Of these, Canada, Australia and China actually assembled Mosquitoes in country. While most countries operated the fighter or fighter-bomber variants of the Mosquito, the following countries flew bomber and/or photo reconnaissance variants:

United States

THe USAAF operated a number of Mosquito variants including the the PR Mk XVI, F-8, and T Mk III. USAAF interest in the Mosquito began with COL Elliott Roosevelt (the President's son) who expressed a desire to obtain Mosquitoes to augment the F-5 Lightning in the long range photo reconnaissance role. The Mosquito was superior to the Lightning in range and ceiling and could carry a 36 inch focal length camera (which the F-5 could not). As a result, GEN Hap Arnold made a formal request for the aircraft and an agreement was reached under which the USAAF would receive 120 aircraft, including ninety from Canada.

During February of 1944, deliveries of an initial batch of twenty Mosquito PR Mk XVIs began to the 8th USAAF in England. The 8th planned on using its Mosquitoes to fill three roles: target weather reconnaissance, night photographic reconnaissance and radar scope photography of selected targets.

The 8th Reconnaissance Weather Squadron (later 653rd Bomb Squadron), 802nd Reconnaissance Group operated the PR Mk XVI in the weather reconnaissance role out of Watton, Norfolk. The aircraft were modified with American radios, instrumentation and a radio altimeter. Flight training for American crews was carried out at Cheddington and the modification work was carried out at Burtonwood. Weather reconnaissance missions involved flying ahead of the bomber formation (usually 10 to 15 minutes) to scout weather, smoke and enemy activity in the target area and relaying the information back to the commander of the bomber force. After one Mosquito was intercepted and shot down by a friendly P-51 Mustang, the unit painted the entire tail surfaces Red as a recognition aid. After the summer of 1944, most weather scouting missions were taken over by P-51s operating in flight strength and the Mosquitoes were used for other more specialized missions.

A requirement to obtain high quality radar scope photography of targets in Germany led to the modification of a number of Mosquito PR Mk XVIs with the H2X radar, a radar scope camera and a 16MM movie camera. The original camera system was later replaced by a K-24 aerial camera mounted directly on the radar scope. The twelve radar conversions were operated by the 654th Bomb Squadron and the 25th Bomb Group and three were lost in action.

The 654th BS also operated eleven PR Mk XVIs modified for the night reconnaissance mission. The modifications included removal of the 58 gallon bomb bay fuel tank, installation of shackles to carry seven M-46 photo flash bombs and the mounting of an American K-19B night camera in the bomb bay just forward of the flash bombs. A second version mounted two K-19Bs, one in the forward bay and a second camera in the rear fuselage. To make up for the loss of internal fuel, 100 gallon underwing slipper tanks were carried as standard.

On 6 October 1944, 8th Air Force officials decided to modify several Mosquitoes for the "Chaff" role. This involved the dropping of metal foil strips to jam German radars. An experimental installation was fitted in the bomb bay of a Mosquito PR Mk XVI which consisted of two eight foot wooden containers that would dispense the strips through metal chutes in the bomb bay doors. Some 600 pounds of Chaff could be carried and dropped by the modified Mosquito. A total of twelve aircraft were converted and operated by the 25th Bomb Group.

Two Mosquitoes were modified under the *Red Stocking* program to serve as radio receiver aircraft for OSS agents operating in occupied Europe. These special operations Mosquitos carried an operator in the bomb bay with a radio and a recorder. A total of four overall Black Mosquitoes were operated under this program by the 492nd Bomb Group.

The U.S. Army Air Force acquired a number of Mosquito PR Mk XVIs for use by the 8th Air Force in England. At least 145 Mosquitoes are known to have served with the 8th Army Air Force, including this PR Mk XVI (NS635). (Harry Holmes)

Sixteen of the ninety Canadian F-8 photo reconnaissance aircraft were dispatched to England for use by the 25th Group. Since these aircraft were variants of the B Mk IV, they were not up to the performance of the PR Mk XVIs then in service, especially in ceiling and range. As a result, the aircraft were never used operationally by the 25th Group. Ten were later transferred to the RAF and the others were returned to the U.S.

Australia

Australia produced the Mosquito under license in two major variants: the fighter-bomber FB Mk 40 and photographic reconnaissance PR Mk 41. The first Australian PR Mosquito was a modified FB Mk 40 that had the guns removed, a three camera reconnaissance installation (two in the nose section and one to the rear of the bomb bay) and extra fuel tanks mounted in the bomb bay (the doors were secured). This aircraft, A52-2, was delivered to No 1 Photographic Reconnaissance Unit, RAAF during May of 1944. At least twenty-four other FB Mk 40s were converted to the PR configuration.

During March of 1944 the unit, now re-designated No 87 (PR) Squadron, received it first Mosquito PR XVI from an order of twelve aircraft purchased from England. Later a second order was placed bringing the total of RAAF PR XVIs to twenty-one. These aircraft remained in service past the end of the war, flying alongside PR Mk 40s and PR Mk 41s.

Because they were basically conversions of FB Mk 40 fighter-bomber airframes that were already on the production line, the PR Mk 41 differed from British built PR variants in that it had a solid nose and a different camera installation. The PR Mk 41 carried a vertical camera under the solid nose, two vertical cameras in the rear fuselage and two oblique cameras, one on each side of the fuselage behind the wing. A total of twenty-eight aircraft were built, serialed A52-300 through A52-327. Most of the PR Mk 41 were used after the war to conduct aerial mapping of the Australian interior. This work was done by both the RAAF Survey Squadron and by civil contract crews flying surplus RAAF Mosquitoes.

A Mosquito PR Mk XVI (NS569/N) of the 546th Bomb Squadron, 8th Air Force shares the rain soaked ramp at Watton with an an unarmed B-17G during 1944. The Mosquito appears to have the name *Camilla* on the nose behind the side window. (Aeroplane)

A Mosquito PR Mk XVI of the 654th Bomb Squadron, 802nd Reconnaissance Group on final approach for landing at an 8th Air Force base in England. The overall PRU Blue aircraft carries Black and White D-Day markings and a Red tail group marking. (AFM via Larry Davis)

Czechoslovakia

A small number of B Mk IVs, along with far greater numbers of FB IVs, were used by No 311 "Atlantic" Squadron, Czech Air Force immediately after the Second World War. These aircraft remained in service until replaced by Soviet built Il-10 ground attack aircraft during the early 1950s.

France

The French Air Force flew the Mosquito PR Mk XVI, PR Mk 23 and PR Mk 34 all of which retained their former RAF serials while in French service. French units flew Mosquitoes in Morocco, Algeria and Indochina. Later, a number of ex-French Mosquitoes were sold to Israel.

Israel

The Israeli Defense Force/Air Force (IDF/AF) flew a mixed force of Mosquitoes including PR Mk XVIs, and at least one B Mk IX. The first Mosquito to enter IDF/AF service was a PR Mk XVI which had been smuggled into Israel in time to see action in the War of Independence (1948/49). During 1950 a number of ex-French Air Force aircraft became available including several PR Mk XVIs. During the 1945-55 period at least fourteen ex-Royal Navy Sea Mosquito TR Mk 33s were sold to the IDF/AF. These aircraft were overhauled in England and all naval equipment was removed. These aircraft saw combat during the Suez Crisis of 1956. During this campaign, the IDF/AF used some eight PR Mosquitoes to photograph Egyptian troop movements and the TR Mk 33 were used in the ground attack role. During its service life with the IDF/AF not one Mosquito was lost in combat, although a number of aircraft were damaged.

The mission markings on the nose of this Mosquito PR Mk XVI of the 654th BS consisted of a Red lightning bolt cutting through a White cloud. The aircraft carries full D-Day markings, a Red tail and Blue spinners. (AFM via Larry Davis).

This Mosquito PR Mk XVI of the 654th BS (R) was modified with an H2X radar set for obtaining radar scope photography of targets in Germany. The radar scope and cameras were set up in the fuselage behind the cockpit and the nose was modified with a large bulbous radome. (AFM via Larry Davis)

South Africa

No 60 Squadron, South African Air Force (SAAF) operated the Mosquito PR Mk IX and XVI from bases in Italy during the later part of the Second World War. The squadron returned to South Africa after the war and conducted aerial mapping of the country using some fourteen PR Mk XVIs.

Soviet Union

A number of ex-RAF B Mk IVs were allocated to the Soviet Union during mid-1944. At least one aircraft was known to have been delivered (DK296) but details of other deliveries are unavailable.

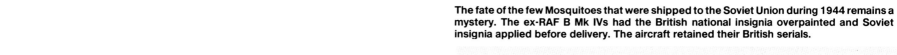

This IDF/AF Mosquito was one of fourteen ex-Royal Navy TR Mk 33s that were overhauled in England and sold to the Israeli Defense Force/Air Force. The aircraft later saw action during the 1956 Suez Crisis. (Aeroplane)

The fate of the few Mosquitoes that were shipped to the Soviet Union during 1944 remains a mystery. The ex-RAF B Mk IVs had the British national insignia overpainted and Soviet insignia applied before delivery. The aircraft retained their British serials.

This Australian-built Mosquito FB 40 (A52-41) was later remanufactured as a PR Mk 41 reconnaissance aircraft. The armament was removed and replaced by cameras. After its conversion the aircraft was reserialed A52-321.

Phase Out

Production of the Mosquito was terminated on 15 November 1950 when the last of 7,781 aircraft (an NF Mk 38) rolled off the de Havilland Chester assembly line. Although this was the end of the production line, foreign orders for reconditioned surplus RAF aircraft kept the de Havilland plant busy in the lean early postwar years.

British postwar use included using Mosquitoes as flying testbeds for numerous weapons and electronics development programs. A number of aircraft were flown by de Havilland and other manufacturers, the Royal Aircraft Establishment and the Aeroplane and Armament Experimental Establishment (Boscombe Down). The Mosquito was used to test weapons, radar and communications equipment. Among the weapons tested was the Uncle Tom rocket. Two of these rockets (about the size of the U.S. 11.75 inch Tiny Tim rocket) could be carried externally under the bomb bay of the Mosquito.

The Mosquito remained in service with the RAF until 1963. That year nine ex-RAF target tugs were passed to a civil company for use in the movie "633 Squadron." The film told the story of the wartime Mosquito crews and was highlighted by some of the best in flight sequences ever put on film. After the filming was completed, one aircraft was selected for permanent display in the Mosquito Museum at Salisbury Hall, alongside the prototype W5040. Another Mosquito FB IV was undergoing restoration and was nearing completion during the Summer of 1992.

In the United States, the Weeks Air Museum has a Mosquito TT 35. This aircraft was built by Airspeed as a B Mk 35 and converted to the TT Mk 35 configuration by Brooklands Aviation during 1951/52. Later the aircraft was used in the movies "633 Squadron" and "Mosquito Squadron." After a lengthy period of storage, the aircraft was restored during 1975 and sold to Kermit Weeks of Miami. The aircraft was repainted in the U.S. to represent the aircraft flown by Group Captain P.C. Pickard during the attack on Amiens prison in 1944.

The Air Force Museum has another Mosquito TT Mk 35. This aircraft has had the bulged bomb bay doors removed and flush doors reinstalled so that the aircraft would more closely represent a PR Mk XVI. After the modification was completed the aircraft was repainted to represent a Mosquito PR Mk XVI of the 25th Bomb Group, 8th Air Force based in England during the Second World War.

The Uncle Tom rocket, an 11 inch unguided air-to-ground weapon, was just one of the weapons tested by the Aeroplane and Armament Experimental Establishment (Boscombe Down) on Mosquito testbeds. The rocket was carried externally under the bomb bay.

The Air Force Museum at Wright Patterson Air Force Base, Dayton, Ohio, has a flyable Moquito TT Mk 35 in its collection. The aircraft was modified with flush bomb bay doors and was repainted to represent one of the PR Mk XVIs flown by the 8th Air Force in England during the Second World War. (D. Menhard via Larry Davis)

This Mosquito TT Mk 35 was built by Airspeed as a B Mk 35 and converted to the target tow configuration by Brooklands Aviation during 1951-52. Later the aircraft was fully restored and was featured in several movies. It is now owned by the Weeks Air Museum of Miami, Florida. (Weeks Air Museum)

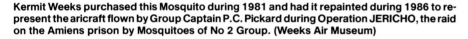

Kermit Weeks purchased this Mosquito during 1981 and had it repainted during 1986 to represent the aricraft flown by Group Captain P.C. Pickard during Operation JERICHO, the raid on the Amiens prison by Mosquitoes of No 2 Group. (Weeks Air Museum)

The Weeks Air Museum Mosquito is a regular at air shows and is one of two flyable Mosquitos in the U.S.(the second is the Air Force Museum's aircraft). The aircraft carries the markings of No 487 Squadron, the unit that led the No 2 Group raid on Amiens prison. (Weeks Air Museum)